TRAPPED BETWEEN YESTERDAY AND TOMORROW

THE HARDEST PLACE IS TO BE IN TODAY

MEGHNA MUKHERJEE

Made with ♥ on the Notion Press Platform
www.notionpress.com

This book is dedicated to my all-time mentor, my father, Mr. Amarnath Mukherjee, who motivated me all the time to pen down my thoughts. He was a hardcore Yoga cum meditation practitioner. No one else knew me better than him. His thirst for knowledge was my biggest inspiration.

Next in line is Dr. Mangesh Bhakre, a general physician. Being a medical practitioner and I a psychologist, we connect on a level beyond words, mainly when it comes to alternative healing.

I would also dedicate this book to my biggest and silent supporter, my mother. Mrs. Anjali mukherjee. She is someone words cannot describe. Without her, I suppose I would be trapped in a dreamy world.

Apart from the above, to my husband, Mr. Niladri Mukherjee, and my brat, Mst. Nimesh Mukherjee, who has been a victim of my emotions, but has stood still waiting for me to come back. Their belief in me is what this book is all about.

A big, big thank you, my dearest family.

Meghna Mukherjee

Contents

Preface *vii*

Introduction To Being Trapped

Part1

1. Why We Replay Old Memories 5
2. The Weight Of Regret 9
3. Grief And Emotional Time Travel 16
4. The Stories We Tell Ourselves 24
5. Memory – Past – Fact File 30

Part 2

6. Why The Brain Predicts Danger? 35
7. My Identity 42

Part 3

8. The Power Of Presence 51
9. Small Steps And Your Relationship With Time. 59
10. Build A Life In The Present 63

Part 4

11. Senses - A Bridge Between You And The World 69

Part 5

12. Returning Home Through The 5 Senses 77

The words of wisdom 79

PREFACE

The first question people will have after reading the title is "WHY"? Why a self-help book dedicated to this topic?

Yet, the question is self-answered. Each one of us is living a life trapped in either the past or the future, yet we live as we say. This book is nothing more than an effort to help readers live in the moment consciously. Mind is a wandered and cannot be caged. What can be done is simply to live the moment consciously.

Honestly, each and every chapter you read will feel as if it is a reality but a reality that you live unknowingly because someway or the oter you are forced back into the present, may be because f the chores. Yet the "ME" time is when the trap encloses, and this book is for that one moement.

Trapped in between today and tomorrow is a mirror to each one of us who are living in denial.

Happy healing to each one of us

Meghna Mukherjee

Introduction to being trapped

A Psychological Guide to Finding Peace in the Present

Imagine waking up every morning carrying two invisible suitcases.

One filled with:

- Regrets
- Losses
- Mistakes
- Pain

The other filled with:

- Worries
- Fears
- What-ifs
- Uncertainty

Most people carry both.

Let's explore how you would unload the suitcases.

Part1

PART I:

THE HOUSE OF YESTERDAY

I

Why We Replay Old Memories

The brain is considered to be a powerhouse of memories. Thinking of something, just press the button and the memory is live as if it is happening now.

Have you ever wondered how you learn a language, or about a flower, or how did you learn about safety from sharp objects or fire? Most importantly, how did you develop yourself? How do you know what kind of person you are? What are your strengths and negatives?

Yes. Absolutely right. The brain has a storage room that has records of all your experiences from the time you are born. And how did you learn all the lessons from?

Senses. Even before you realised, your senses have started making sense out of the world around you. The senses are a bridge between us and the world. A bridge we have formed unknowingly and continue to form through experiences and revisiting our memories.

Relax and Replay

The brain does not need an instruction to play or be active. While you are eating or talking on the phone or simply sky gazing, the brain is playing some or the other memory that connects you with yourself and the world around. Or else, just think, you are running on a busy road, yet you monitor your movements and avoid accidents. How? It's simply the brain doing its homework. Through your senses, the brain has recorded an event of safety that alerts you to your move simply. Take any situation where you have simply been successful, and you will notice how something unknowingly in the recorded past saves you at the moment. But sometimes, on-the-spot recall does not happen, and you simply regret your actions.

The day ends, but not for the brain. The brain is actively playing on some past, and it either makes you happy or sad while revisiting the memory. Mainly after a terrible day, say you had a terrible day at work, lots of pressure, or could not meet the deadline, or colleagues just did not cooperate, and you had a verbal fight. Just before you hit the bed, the brain recalls an event, good and bad. Which one do you hold on to? Depending on how you wish to view yourself, you will project yourself accordingly.

But wait....

- Did the brain just provoke me/you?
- What and why is it playing a part of me that is somehow connected with me and makes me feel good and bad at the same time?
- Is the brain playing a game with me, you?

The answer is simply, "NO"

The brain is neither playing a game nor did it provoke you nor point to the bad in you. It is simply trying to protect you from the emotional trauma you are replaying in your head.

The event in your office has traumatised you, and you are feeling terrible about it. You do not wish to discuss it with anyone at home or with friends, and instead of tearing up, you tend to put up a strong front, but internally, it is eating you up. At this time, who can help you? You, yourself. That is what the brain is doing. It is playing a memory where you can find answers to your issue. Or it plays a memory where you were less burdened and happy-go-lucky. Also, it tells you that everything seemed good, but you were strong and dealt with issues at that time, smiling. So, it's up to you to deal with the current situation as well. Take an excerpt from the past, implement, and move on. Humans evolved to remember painful experiences because remembering mistakes helped us survive.

Unfortunately, the brain cannot always distinguish between:

- Learning from the past
- Living in the past

Many people think they revisit painful memories because they haven't "gotten over them."

In reality, they often revisit them because their mind is still searching for a resolution.

Consider a woman who lost a job unexpectedly. Years later, she still thinks about it. Not because she enjoys suffering. Because part of her mind keeps asking:

- What did I do wrong?
- Could I have prevented it?
- What if I had spoken up?
- What if I had chosen differently?

The brain loves unanswered questions. It treats them like unfinished business.

Rumination VS Worry

As said earlier. The brain does the act of protecting you, but how one responds to the memory plays a crucial role. Living and recalling the past creates a sense of nostalgia. If given a choice, I would love to live like a child, carefree and taken care of. Remunerating the lovely childhood days brings a sense of nostalgia (feeling happy and positive), but think practically

- Can we get back to those days now?

Practically being impossible, the brain takes us to those nostalgic moments, live them, and rejuvenates us. But for some people, pain is unbearable, and they retreat to their past. They are stuck in the past, and whenever stressed, they retreat to their happy days and wish to live in that situation or try to create a similar situation, which is practically impossible.

Nostalgia is generally positive. Yet researchers believe that experiencing nostalgia may involve elements of sadness as people miss parts of their past. This is the time when people experience sadness, often referred to as "Nostalgic depression" (though not a diagnosis), which describes negative emotions that people feel when thinking about their past. It may refer to sadness in contrast to happier memories, with present negative feelings. It can also mean longing for the past but feeling negative emotions when someone is unable to reclaim it.

Studies suggest that people may focus on negative memories when experiencing nostalgia. They can exclude positive aspects of the same memories. If a person perceives their past as happier than their present, they may feel emotional distress, leading to symptoms of depression. Researchers also mentioned that nostalgia could lead people to worry and ruminate more. Rumination is when a person repeatedly thinks about or dwells on negative feelings and their causes and consequences.

The mind continues returning to these moments because it believes another visit might finally produce the answer. But repeatedly opening the same emotional wound does not necessarily help it heal. Sometimes understanding comes from acceptance.

Reflection Exercise

Write down:

- The memory visited most often.
- What is your learning from it that the brain is recalling?

Healing begins when we don't say,
"Why did this happen?"
but saying
"What can I learn from this?"

II

The Weight of Regret

- "If I had"
- "Only if I had done this or that"
- "I wish I knew"
- "Oh, how I wish I could do something about it"

I am sure all of us are aware of these words and are using them all the time, consciously or subconsciously. These are the words used mainly when we see our ball in another court, or a dream not fulfilled, or the success parameter is too high, whereby expectations are unmet.

We know that, whatever the situation, we can add "if" or "may be "connotations.

- Academics. A degree one wanted/expected percentage
- Job or an opportunity lost.
- Business
- Love life
- Marriage

And the list goes on and on.... Every situation where the desire is unmet or unfulfilled is when regret steps in. One of the most misunderstood emotions is regret. As per the layman's term, regret stems from making mistakes or from unfulfilled desires and outcomes. Simply put, regret often comes from being human.

The Ghost of the Unlived LIFE

Being human, we have a choice. A choice creating two lives:

- The life we lived.
- The life we didn't.

All of us are breathing a living example of the first choice. The role we are currently playing is the choice we have made, and we are living it every moment. The second life exists only in imagination. Yet it can feel surprisingly real.

- A woman who didn't become a doctor imagines the doctor she might have been.
- A man who ended a relationship imagines the marriage that might have happened.

The imagined life often appears perfect because reality never had the opportunity to complicate it.

Regret is one of the heaviest emotions a person carries because it asks us to do something impossible. "It asks us to change the past." And no matter how hard we try, the past can be remembered but cannot be changed.

As said earlier, the second life, the life we never lived, seems fascinating. It is a road that we have never walked, yet it seems that the road would have been easier, simply full of opportunities waiting for us, and we would have succeeded and become the person we dreamt of becoming. The unimagined or unlived life becomes a reality and is easy to walk on as it was in the past, and we are creating a new path standing from the present road where we are present. The unlived life has a powerful advantage over reality. It never has to deal with real problems. In our imagination, the alternative path often becomes perfect.

- We imagine success without struggle.
- Love without conflict.
- Achievement without sacrifice.

Whereas Reality never receives the same generous treatment.

- Reality contains bills, disappointments, setbacks, uncertainty, complexity, and the burden of the current life.

ꟷ

Why Regret stabs hard?

Regret is not a standalone emotion. Along with regret, we carry emotions like

- Grief
- Hope
- Disappointment
- Anger
- Guilt

Now imagine a gush of varied emotions. One feels the pinch, the pain, and it is quite humanly we can never see ourselves in a faded light. The guilt is too high for rejecting the easier life. What is the defence mechanism one would play to protect oneself? Exactly, "If only I had chosen differently."

But only if life were that simple and realistic....

Every choice we make is like the two sides of a coin—having advantages and disadvantages. When faced with regret, the current life seems to be a disadvantage, and the unwalked road or choices seem advantageous. This creates a distorted comparison. We compare our real life to an imaginary one. And imaginary lives almost always win.

Just like the "Grass is greener on the other side"

Owning the wisdom to save us

Once we have reached where we are, we acquire knowledge either by interacting with others or through the newspapers and other sources of information. The bank of knowledge we generate makes us now a learned individual. This is where we humans are at fault. The human mind is judging past decisions using present knowledge.

Think: You know things today that you did not know five or ten years ago. You have different experiences and perspectives now. Yet many people evaluate their past choices as though they should have possessed today's wisdom back then.

They say: "I should have known."

"But pause, really, could you? Could the younger version of you have known what only experience could teach?

Our choices at that time were based on certain perspectives that seemed real at that point in time. Eg, Rajesh, a middle-class bank manager, wanted to start a business. He shared his idea with a friend who is currently successful. Rajesh looks back and feels that he should have continued with his idea of starting a business. Yet what he needs to think is that, at that time, he was 30 years old married man with a child whose future was in his hands. He needed to save rather than get into something risky. Today, being well settled, he regrets his past decision of not starting a business. But, in realty could he invest in the unknown? It wasn't careless. It was reasonable based on the circumstances he faced. His regret came from a confusing outcome. The outcome turned out differently than he had hoped. That doesn't automatically mean the decision was wrong. This realization changed his mindset about himself. He stopped judging his younger self harshly. And in doing so, he began to experience peace.

The Difference Between Regret and Responsibility

Many people fear that letting go of regret means avoiding responsibility.

Ponder on the following statements:

- Responsibility says: "I made a mistake."
- Regret often says, "I am a mistake."

The 1st statement allows one to take responsibility and grow, while the 2nd statement fills one with guilt or regret, which makes one suffer.

Regret teaches us

Sometimes regret isn't actually about the event itself. It is about a deeper meaning, a deeper need that is hidden subconsciously.

A woman may regret not becoming a doctor. But what she truly misses might be:

- Purpose.
- Contribution.
- Growth.
- Achievement.
- Recognition.

Those needs may still be available to her today, taking a different profession. The dream of being a doctor has been replaced by her being a teacher, but the needs remain. This is an important distinction. Because when people focus only on the lost opportunity, they feel powerless. When they identify the need beneath it, possibilities return. Perhaps you cannot return to the past. But you may still create meaning in the present.

Perfect Decision – A myth

Humans love to be perfect. Everything associated with them has to be perfect. "The Perfect ME" People spend their lives searching for the one perfect decision. Some continue achieving degree after degree. What kind of perfection are they searching for? Is that achievable?

The perfect career, partner, investment, opportunity, and so on. The perfect timing. But life rarely offers certainty. Most decisions are made with incomplete information. We first make a choice, followed by discovery. The latter does not happen. We are uncertain and not perfect before making a decision. This means uncertainty is not evidence of failure. It is part of being human. No one gets to see both futures before making a choice. Everyone chooses while being partially blind. Some choices work beautifully. Others don't. Both experiences teach and shape us and make us the person we are today.

Defence-Mechanism: Self-Forgiveness

Since humans wish to be perfect and are in search of perfectionism, they start the self-blame game. Whereas the underlying fact is certainty. Every decision is made first, and then one can see the outcome. In this scenario, humans need to deal with regret. The only self-defence humans have is to ponder on their decision, weigh its pros and cons, and practice "forgiveness". One of the greatest acts of emotional maturity is learning to forgive the person you used to be.

Not because they were perfect. Not because they never made mistakes. But because they were doing the best they could with the awareness they had at the time. Self-forgiveness does not erase accountability. It simply removes unnecessary cruelty.

Many people speak to themselves in ways they would never speak to someone they love. Imagine sitting across from your younger self. Perhaps twenty years old naïve self. You are able to see the confusion and fear on your face. Now:

- Would you attack yourself?
- Or would you offer understanding?

Most of us know how to offer compassion to others. The challenge is learning to extend that same compassion inwards.

Reflection Exercise

In a journal, write:

"I still regret..."

Then answer these questions:

1. What did I know at that time?
2. What pressure or challenges did I face at that time?
3. What need was I trying to fulfil at that time?
4. What lessons have I learned by making a decision?

At the end, whatever the decision and the outcome, write and say loudly to yourself. Repeat 3 times.

"I forgive myself for not knowing what only time could teach."

It will not be accepted at one go, but eventually it sinks in.

III

Grief and Emotional Time Travel

When the Heart Lives in a Different Time Zone

Imagine a foggy day. You are surrounded by dense fog, whereby you wish to see beyond, but the fog is blocking your vision and making you feel uncomfortable. You wish to get rid of the fog, and suddenly you see a silver lining and the clear sky. Grief is like the fog. It envelopes you till you cannot see anything beyond. But as said, every dark cloud has a silver lining. Even grief has an end. Only the person grieving knows when and how.

Defining Grief?

Grief is not all about forgetting or learning to live in the moment. In simple words, the world around us moves. The sun rises and sets, time passes, schools and offices are functional, and the moments are all around us, but the person grieving is stuck in a moment.

- Waiting for just a call
- Waiting for one final touch or talk
- Resignation / Termination call

- Divorce or the end of a relationship

It's like two timelines exist at one point in time. One where everything is moving forward, and one where time is stuck for the person in grief. Please note that time just does not stand still. It moves, but flashback keeps coming and going, and at that time, everything stands still.

For the person in grief, life is divided into two phases:

- Life before
- Life after

The present life does not exist. The life before phase, which was initially ordinary, suddenly becomes extraordinary. Small things that initially did not matter suddenly become important, and the person keeps revisiting them.

- Sitting with a cup of tea on a windowsill
- Discussions over a newspaper
- Small corrections that at that time irritated us, but now are missed

I recall, when I was grieving and missing my father, I would simply go and sit on a couch at the corner of the room, thinking that he is still there and I am hugging him, and wept like a baby. It's not grief but the value that grief teaches us about the person. We start valuing everything the person did or said. It's a human tendency to value something after it's gone. When it is with us, we barely bother or give it importance. This is the main reason why grief affects us more than anything. And we are stuck at one moment, the past or the life lived before.

Eg: All of us are busy in our lives, and once we mature or once we have kids, we know most things. A simple piece of advice from our parents seems to be nagging and interference. We rebuke them for their unnecessary advice, stating, "Our times are different." Or "you just don't understand. Don't interfere." Yet today, when the person has passed away, we miss those small pieces of advice that we took as interferences. It is the regret that causes grief while we are trying to recover from the loss.

Refusal to accept reality

The strangest part of grief is "acceptance of reality," whereby one knows that physically the person or object is gone, yet cannot accept it. They keep waiting and attach meaning to them.

- The loved one has passed away, but still, one feels that the door will open and they will walk in
- The relationship is over, yet they feel that the phone will ring or a message will come, and things will be back to normal.
- One has lost a job, yet they feel that they will be called back.

Psychologists sometimes refer to this as a gap between cognitive understanding and emotional acceptance. In layman's terms, a fight between emotions and logic.

The heart is a whirlpool of emotions and sometimes can be overpowered when the situation is tense. The mind logically accepts, but the heart does not accept, and this creates an internal conflict. This is where the grief turns into something beyond. The mind keeps visualising things in a positive way as if things are turning in the favour of the aggrieved person. They are unable to differentiate between reality and imagination, and they feel safeguarded in their virtual reality world, unable to accept reality, which is harsh.

Memories become intense. You start noticing intricate details that earlier went unnoticed.

- Smell of the perfume
- The way someone called out your name
- A particular phrase, song, or dance

Why does memory become so intense as if it's happening right in front of us? A virtual reality or photogenic memory is activated, safeguarding the person from trauma and, more importantly, losing oneself. It's like a rewind and play button that is activated, helping to keep the person sane.

Ever wondered why we hold on to

- Mementos/letters/pens
- Video recordings/photos

- Voice messages
- Perfume bottle
- Watch

It is not the value we assign to the objects, but the connection. We have lost the person physically, so connections are broken, but the objects are now a connection with the person. We revisit them so that the connection is not broken once and for all.

Eg, Remember Kareena Kapoor from 3 idiots wearing her mother's watch. The only connection left with her mother. Grief is nothing more than the fear of losing the connection once and for all. It is simply saying, "We are grieving, but we have moved on."

The Empty Nest Syndrome:

Who said grief is only about bereavement or death? It can even be a small change or shift.

Changes due to

- Marriage
- Children moving out for studies/a job
- Longing for the old self
- Quitting a job.
- Divorce

Change is mandatory and keeps happening, and a necessity. But longing and attachment towards anything leads to regret and unacceptance, leading to revisiting the past, leading to grief. Grief is all about accepting the change and moving ahead with the new self.

"Empty nest syndrome" refers to a situation where children move out for studies or a job, but the mother is unable to accept the change and longs for her child. She clings to some objects of the past, thinking the child is with her. It is a syndrome stating that change is unacceptable, leading to grief.

Emotional Time Travel

Life is a journey, and we are travellers exploring different aspects of life. Simply like a train passing through every station. Life is like a train, and we are like the bogies trudging along the way, gaining exposure and experiences that shape how we see life. The train is on the track called life's journey, and the stations represent chapters of life. Each chapter represents

- childhood days,
- adulthood,
- marriage
- Job
- Relationship
- Self-journey
- Children
- Old age

Every chapter teaches us something. Some we learn while some we ignore. Simply put, when we are on a tour, we have an itinerary. We try our best to visit all the places in the itinerary while some are missed. As the train keeps moving, we move, but our hearts, being emotional, feel the gap and fill us with regret, leading to grief. It is then that we keep revisiting them and try to mend them. Sometimes it is possible, while sometimes we create virtual reality, trying to keep ourselves safe and protected from the grief arising due to incomplete or left-over tasks. It is the virtual reality that needs to be checked, or one will learn to live with grief in its own ways. The body continues moving, but the heart stays behind, longing for closure. This creates emotional suffering because life requires participation. And participation can only happen in the present.

Resisting the Healing process

When in grief, our well-wishers say," Move on." The question is, move on from what?

- From the person
- Change
- The fear
- Happiness

It's easier said than done. Grief is more than sadness. Sit over grooming and then move on with life, but grief is not helping someone to move on. Grief accompanies guilt.

People resist healing or trying to overcome grief mainly because

- **Fear.** They fear that if they heal, they will lose the connection forever. Sometimes, or rather most of the time, we all have unfinished tasks, but one cannot keep regretting the unfinished. They have to move on or stay punished in grief, losing their present due to the past.
- **What will people say**? Sometimes, just to let society know how much we are connected with the person, we prefer showing our emotional side. But how much do people care? It's all about ourselves and our connection with the person. Care and love cannot be shown. Only felt.
- **A betrayal.** The belief is that the more you grieve or cry or feel sad, the more you care, or else you are selfish.

Half the time, people are thinking about others and their thoughts and trying to be the best person in the eyes of the society. This pushes people into psychological issues that cannot heal. People prefer the past, whereby they feel protected, forgetting that being in the present is healing by itself naturally.

Learning to Love Differently

People carry a myth that clinging or holding on means love. Is it love or pain? Love and pain are two different things. Pain reflects loss, while love reflects a connection even after the loss.

Healing happens when things are viewed differently. Imagine, would your loved one like to see you in pain, in grief, or in a state of sadness all the time? Remember, healing does not happen when you punish yourself, or by not being able to forget, or by pretending. Healing happens when you learn to love but love differently.

Imagine grief as a suitcase that you are carrying. Initially, it is heavy because of carrying the burden of guilt, pretending, and many other negativities. It feels heavy, needing both your hands to lift the suitcase. Now eliminate the guilt and other negativity. The suitcase is lighter. Not because the contents are removed but because the way you see things has changed. A change in perspective and idea. The memory remains, but the way you deal with it changes. You start becoming stronger by keeping the memories intact. What changes is your relationship with them. You no longer carry the grief, but you carry the love. A different form of love. Grief is not about forgetting but learning to carry love differently.

Realization: The 1st step towards healing

Realizing a few facts starts the healing process

- My loved ones would never like to see me in pain or sadness
- One bad chapter in a book does not define the entire book.
- My past does not define my present nor future.

This realization is like a permission. A permission that everything is well, and one needs to let the sunshine shine brightly, as life in me is still breathing.

Reflection Exercise

Close your eyes and think of someone you have lost, a loved one.

Now ask yourself: What am I grieving, the person, the relationship, or the identity I lost, or the connection?

Now answer: How would you heal, without forgetting the person?

"Healing is not forgetting, but healing is forgetting by not being imprisoned by memory. "

IV

The Stories We Tell Ourselves

A Bridge between creating and suffering

Note, the event is not a wound, but the story around it makes the event a wound.

Imagine yourself standing in front of a mirror. What do you see? Would you see another you created by a mirror or your own reflection? Obviously, your reflection. Just as you are.

The point to be noted here is that the mind never creates on its own. It absorbs and then deducts meaning. Most importantly, it creates a story based on what has been fed to it. Just like feeding data into the computer, fetching an outcome. You feed negativity, positivity cannot be birthed. It's like the proverb, "What you sow, so shall you reap"

Life is full of events. Thousands of events are happening and are being recorded.

- Someone didn't reply to your message
- A family member forgot your birthday or anniversary
- A colleague did not reciprocate and just walked by
- A plan was cancelled by a friend/family member

These are mere events that can happen to anyone. But immediately, the mind starts creating an explanation. Mind is someone who cannot accept anything and lingers over it again and again. It wants a closure. So, the explanation it creates would be based on past experiences, and a story is born. Since the story is based on certain criteria, they become a reality. One then starts believing them and what you believe becomes an identity. And thus, the mere event turned into an identity that the person carries all along.

The Story created through the lens

Imagine two friends seeing the world through two different coloured lenses – blue and green. For one child, the world is blue, and for the other it is green. It is their perception that they framed through the lens they have seen the world through. As said before, life is full of chapters creating different experiences. Different experiences are seen through different lenses. Lens-like:

- Childhood
- Success/failure
- Beliefs
- Cultural expectations
- Relationship

Every experience adds a new lens, and we keep adding. The challenge here is to remove the previous lens/experience before adding a new lens/experience. We add a new experience or lens to the already existing lens, which then becomes grounded. Point to be noted here is that, if the glass of the window you see the world through is not clear and you see the world without cleaning it, what will you notice? What is the belief you will carry? What is the story created? Similarly, unless and until the past lenses are worked upon, the new lens would project a similar view.

The Story we created as children

Imagine an 8-year-old girl who was asked by the teacher to read a paragraph from a book. She was nervous and hence spelled a word wrong. Her classmates laughed at her. The teacher corrected her. The teacher moved on with her teaching. The incident lasted for a minute. The teacher forgot the incident after correcting the child. Her classmates forgot about the incident as soon as the school day ended. As for the little girl, she created a story. A story that will haunt her growth in the near future.

Next time, when she is asked to read in front of the class. The story created by her would be: "It is dangerous to read before others. What if I make a mistake again and others laugh?"- Fear and Self-consciousness.

A few years later, the story goes: "Public speaking is not for me."

The ordinary event evolved into a lifetime of disaster just because of the meaning associated with it, which turned into a belief embedded in the system.

Identity created through a Story

Can you tell the difference between

- I failed
- I am a failure

"I failed" is an event. Many times, we fail depending on the set parameters and the efforts we took.

"I am a failure," An identity I give myself. I associate myself with the failure and identify myself as a failure.

Every event we participate in does not mean we have to be successful. Some are good with sports, some with studies, while some are good or natural when it comes to relationships. But a failure in one's life, one creates a belief, a story, and then identifies and self-blames oneself, saying, "I am a failure." Many mental health issues begin when experiences turn into an identity.

- A divorce means, "I am not lovable"
- A job loss means, "I am good at nothing"

- A rejection means, "I am not wanted by anyone"

The event ends, but the identity remains. Hence, many times the wound hurts long after the event has happened. The mind repeats the story whenever a similar kind of event occurs. As said before, the mind cannot accept uncertainty. It wants a closure. So, any hurtful event, the mind starts associating with a story, and an identity is created, which hurts the person emotionally, leading to psychological issues later.

Imagine a child who looks at his father for affection. Father is someone who has lots of love in him but cannot show it by hugging or through words. What happens to the child?

The child does not understand the way human functions. Yet he wants an answer, an explanation to calm down his questioning mind. After a few similar experiences, he creates a story, "If my father does not show me love, something may be wrong with me." This story is grilled as a mindset and a failure in love life, which will grill the story as an identity.

The midlife crisis turned into a story

When people enter their forties and above, new events lead to the formation of a new story, leading to a new identity.

Story 1: Most common, "It's too late"

- I wish I had started earlier
- The opportunity has passed now. No use trying now
- I am pretty old now

What is the age to learn, grow, or start something new? Many dreams die not because one is old or has no time, but due to the story associated with it.

Story 2: The comparison story.

Seeing others' love life, marriage, relationship, home, job, etc., one starts comparing oneself to them and silently whispers, "I am way behind them"

Why do we believe in a negative story?

Have you noticed the brain replaying negativity when someone is sad or feeling low? It's like adding fuel to one's sadness and igniting it. Any idea why? Simply, the brain has evolved towards threats. By accepting criticism, the brain protects itself as it can relate to an identity. Hence, the hurt is bearable.

Make a note; we accept criticism easily while slowly accepting praise. Someone compliments you; you dismiss it, while someone criticizes you, you remember it for years. As a result, we humans are experts in collecting evidence of criticism. If need be, we can give a list of criticisms immediately, but ask for moments or words of praise, and we hardly recall any.

We remember and recollect easily:

- Failures
- Criticism
- Rejection
- Mistakes

We conveniently forget:

- Events we dealt with resilience
- Our achievements
- Our strengths
- Kindness
- Growth and success

Note how these stories feel like facts, yet they are interpretations, not facts. Repeated thoughts do feel like reality. It's like a replay, but it does not have a bit of truth in it.

An Author in the making

A pseudo-author has been writing your story till now. Since they did not know anything good about you, they were filling the chapters with only negatives about you and creating a wrong identity. Now imagine you have the ink in your hand, and you have been asked to pen down chapters of your life. You wish to give it another ending. What will you pen down? What will the ending be?

If I were the author, I would include and visualize myself as:

- A survivor
- An adaptor to various situations
- The times I kept going despite setbacks
- The times I tried despite no support and fear of society

If Life is my identity, then why associate it with only negative stories, when I have been standing strong against the winds, which must be mentioned. Don't wait for life to change. Instead, change the story. A change in story will change your behavior and your attitude, creating a new you. A new identity.

Reflection Exercise

In your journal, ask yourself and write:

The story I tell myself?

When did the story begin?

Evidence for and against the story?

If you are writing a new story. What would it be?

V

Memory – Past – Fact file

Before we conclude the prognosis based on identity or ruminating or grief and connection to the loved one, we lost. Let's understand what the recollection of the past is trying to say to us.

Before the prognosis, let us answer a simple question. When do we race back to our memories? When does it haunt us?

One of the answers is when we are recovering from grief. But what in grief keeps us grounded to the past, not letting us live in the present? Simple, grief is a profound emotion and quite unbearable. Many a time, you may have seen a grieved person crying or shouting like a baby, avoiding food, and acting clumsily. Mostly out of life. The mind or the brain wants to protect the self from harm and hence retreats back to the past, good memories.

Dwelling on the happy memory during the mourning or grief period is the best way to recover, but the issue is when the person stops living in the moment and is stuck in the past, which is more like a comfort zone. This is where grief turns grave. Grief turns into depression, whereby the person does not wish to move ahead. They assume the imaginary world or the already happened world as the current world.

I had a client who lost her mother, and being the only child was not available to help her mother during her sickness. This guilt stayed with her and grew bigger after the mother passed away suddenly after a prolonged illness. She was unable to accept her not being a responsible girl. When she missed her mother, she returned to the good olden days when she would support and care for her mother. She was depressed and found refuge in her past good old memory.

Another answer is when someone is stressed or in a painful situation and wants closure to their suffering. When you are hurt, what do you do? Just cry over the wound or opt for healing? Obviously healing. When you were hurt as a child, you went to your mother, who hugged you and calmed you down, relieving you of the pain. Now, as a grown-up, can you take shelter in your mother's lap? Relieving the past is like a shelter in your mother's lap, but instead of fighting the stress, you search for a recluse retreating to the past, which is where it turns into something painful. Living in the past, ignoring the present, is a symptom of depression that needs attention immediately.

Remember, the past is our safe house where we take shelter to calm our present, but staying too much in the past, ignoring healing, is something one needs to be cautious about.

Part 2

PART II:

THE LAND OF TOMORROW

VI

Why the Brain Predicts Danger?

All of us have faced one or many crises in our lives.

- Heavy rains / or any calamity, and a loved one's phone is unreachable
- Loud noise
- Lightning sounds and gushing winds like a storm
- Sound of the rustling leaf.

You may question. All these are normal events. Obviously, during the rainy season, lightning and storm situations happen. Big deal, but the instances are mentioned in terms of waiting for a loved one or stressed about an exam or a job, or even planning a trip. As said earlier, the brain searches for an answer, a closure. It is simply trying to reduce the stress and protect the human. Hence, the first anticipatory response to the above situations is "threat." The brain assumes danger and alerts us, creating panic, and humans are geared up to protect themselves and others.

Research has proven that for humans, assuming danger is safer than assuming a no-threat situation, as it prepares the body for a fight or flight situation, whichever is applicable. But instead, if we anticipate safety, the body is relaxed, and in case the situation is threatening, action would be delayed.

Eg, You are trekking in a jungle. History has taught us that the jungle is home to wild animals. It's nighttime. Visibility is affected or low. Suddenly, you hear the rustling of leaves as if someone is approaching. The mind assumes it's a wild animal and all the protective gears are in hand. The rustling of the leaves could have been just the leaves swaying against the wind, but the mind assumed a wild animal. Why? Simply, because it prepared the body for the worst. If one assumed the wind and kept walking without any weapon and was attacked by a wild animal, it could have been fatal. Hence, the brain alerts us more to danger than to safety.

What is the primary objective of the brain? Neither fulfilment nor confidence nor happiness nor success. Throughout history, the primary objective of the brain has been "survival." Think about how did our ancestors who lived in jungles survived and evolved? The invention of weapons, clothes, and fire are all examples of how they were invented for survival. If they had not survived, generations over generations would not have come.

The mantra of survival passed on from our ancestors still exists in us. The brain has evolved and adapted to those changes. The issue is that the world has changed drastically while the brain is slow. Today, the danger is different. They are more:

- Psychological
- Uncertainty
- Stress – Finance, education, career, relationship
- Failures and success
- Comparison
- Competition

Yet the way the brain works is the pre-old ways only. It assumes that there is danger, and safety protocol is alerted.

The Brain's purpose

Suppose if the brain were given a choice. A choice between

- Keeping you happy/comfortable
- Keeping you alive/safe

What will the brain choose? The brain functions to keep humans safe, despite what the human wants – happiness. The brain cannot differentiate between happiness and safety. It assumes that being safe is being happy.

Eg: The recent Mumbai train attacks. You were travelling in the train, but you survived the attack, and you are happy. The brain registered that being safe in the attack made you happy. So next time, when faced with a similar situation, say the stress of an exam. It will try to protect or make you safe, which eventually will make you happy. Even if the safety creates discomfort. This is the beginning of anxiety. Assuming something negative during unforeseen circumstances is something that psychologists define as "anticipatory anxiety"

The Smoke Detector Analogy – Overreacting to Simple Situations

Ponder on the commonly used statements:

- It's not a life and death situation, I know, yet it feels like one
- I know, I will survive. It's not the end of the road

These feelings help people to take actions they may not regret, but they act in haste to diminish the intensity of the strongly felt emotions; no matter what, the outcome is definitely unpleasant.

Imagine installing a smoke detector at home. When will it ring, when there is smoke due to a burnt toast, or when the house is on fire? The smoke detector does its duty, smoke emitting from a burnt toast, is smoke and detecting it, it would ring, but what if it does not ring when the house is on fire? Though inconvenient, it still rings and protects us. This is what is called a "false alarm," but it does the same work. Situations create anticipatory anxiety, raising a false alarm, but it is at this time that the brain, to protect us, sets off in action.

Daniel Goleman, the renowned expert on emotional intelligence, offered a potent analogy for understanding anxiety: "Anxiety is the mind's smoke detector – sometimes it warns of real danger, but often it's just burnt toast.

The "smoke alert analogy" is a powerful psychological tool explaining anxiety and the physical distress as protective alarm systems. Just as a smoke detector beeps for burnt toast instead of a real house fire, our brain sometimes triggers a fight-or-flight response.

Anxiety is nothing but a perceived reality or an anticipation of the worst. Anxiety always works on the imagination of unforeseen situations. The brain prefers an unnecessary warning (false alarm) rather than missing a genuine issue. Hence, you feel panic or anxiety before:

- A presentation
- A job interview
- An exam

Since it is a new situation, the brain perceives a threat and raises an alarm, not because the events are dangerous, but because they are new; one can view them as perceived threats. So, protection is better. The problem is not with minor anxiety like uneasiness or a growling stomach, but when anxiety becomes chronic. For those living with chronic anxiety, Goleman says, "The constant barrage of anxious thoughts, physical sensations, and anticipatory dread makes it incredibly difficult to discern between genuine threats and the mind's overactive imagination. " One of the favourite activities of the brain is imagining the worst-case scenario. Psychologists call this the catastrophising effect. It's as simple as "a small concern, but the brain has reached countless steps ahead. Long jump scenario"

Eg: You have a headache.

Someone suffering from chronic anxiety will catastrophise the situation. Say, after taking medicines, the pain still does not subside, the person starts sweating, and thinks

- What if I have some underlying issue?

He or she may start surfing the net for symptoms and causes, and his or her imagination leads to the worst scenario

- What if I have a major illness and am about to die soon?

Since it is imagined, the future never happens, but the body reacts as if it is happening, and they can foresee it.

Anxiety – Uncertainty

Ask a layman, what is anxiety, and how does it stem from? The answer simply would be that anxiety stems from events and our imagination. But anxiety stems not from events but from not knowing what the event entails for us in the future.

Eg. A job interview. The candidate is unsure what the outcome would be. Would they be selected? What will be the questions asked? And many more.....

This unknown future creates uncertainty, and one suffering from chronic anxiety will create an entire movie out of it. All thanks to the brain. As said earlier, the brain wants closure.

The brain asks: "What happens next?"

Life answers: "We will soon find out"

This gap, where the mind creates answers of its own, mainly negative, is where anxiety dwells.

Travelling to the future

If depression is due to the past, anxiety is in terms of anticipation of the future. An anxious person often questions, "What will happen?" Anxiety lives in possibilities, and possibilities thrive on imagination. Anticipating the future leads to anxiety. The mind keeps creating scenarios that never happen in reality, but drains the person till the outcome.

Eg: Imagine you have a speech to give. You prepare for the event, but before that, while preparing, you create countless scenarios

- What if I forget what I have to say?
- What if the audience mocks me?
- What if I appear foolish in front of everyone?
- Will I be able to do public speaking in the future?

You are panicking till you are on the stage. Luckily, the speech goes well. All applaud you, and that brings a smile to your face. The result does not matter here; the question here is:

- How long did you suffer for a 20-minute speech?
- Was it worth it?

Stressful weeks of preparation for 20 minutes of reality. What cost does one pay for anxiety? As said, we often suffer longer from an imagined future than the actual event.

Calming the brain

The anxious brain believes, "If I predict danger in advance, I will be safe."

Uncertainty is obvious, as the future is something that no one can see. Hence, worrying about the future creates panic. It's like, "the fear of the unknown." The goal is not to create certainty but to become capable. Capable of handling every situation as and when it arises. It is a mindset. Easier said than done.

Instead of saying, "How can I make sure everything goes perfectly"

Say, "Am I well equipped to handle challenges as they arise"

Reflection Exercise

In your journal:

Whenever you notice anxiety, write: What am I predicting and its outcome?

At the end of the week, review your predictions.

VII

My Identity

"Fear is something we experience, but that is not the danger. The danger is when we begin to perceive or feel we are one with the fear"

Each one of us might have seen or experienced

- Nail biting/skin peeling by oneself
- Extra talking / Loudly speaking
- Pacing around the room
- Fidgety
- Restlessness
- Looking at the time continuously
- Staring at a place unknowingly
- Difficulty sleeping

These are nothing but signs of fear or anxiety, which is common. It is a sense of survival. A bit of anxiety is needed or is a boost to survival and making the right decision, but too much, which we call chronic anxiety, or associating every situation and oneself with the fear of the situation, which is alarming. Being aware of such a happening is what this book is all about.

The Invisible Prison:

Notice the difference in the saying:

"I am an anxious person"

"I feel anxious"

"I am a worrier"

I feel worried"

Feeling an emotion is like an experience. We feel many things, turning them into an experience. When one personalizes it, saying, "me", "I", "am", they start identifying with it. Gaining experience is good, but identifying with it is definitely an issue in the long run. It simply means labelling oneself. Once someone identifies or labels themselves, they start living it every moment, and it becomes a part of them consciously.

We identify with our name, our job title. Once an identity is formed and one identifies with it, it becomes difficult to breathe. It's like pulling a fish out of water. It's like an identity card or a badge we carry around. It defines us, as in who we are. And how we wish to be seen or perceived. It turns into our story, titled "This is ME." It is an unseen cage around us, as if someone has tied us with a rope and we are stuck with it.

Exercise: Continuously, say to yourself, "I am...." either positive words or negative words. After a few days, you will start identifying yourself with the "I am..." statement.

When we are born, we come with nothing. No name, no identity. Then how do we form an identity? It is as simple as when someone calls me by a particular name, I respond and am acknowledged for it. That is how we know our name, which is an identity for us. Then how do we identify with our emotions?

A child is like a blank slate or like a sponge. What you write, or you drill into him or her, they start forming their identity accordingly.

As Eric Berne mentioned in the book, "Games people play," The child is small and is afraid of a huge figure called the parent or an adult. When he knows nothing good or bad, whatever the parent or the adult tells him becomes a deadline, and it is engraved into him. He then gets an identity.

A child who worries excessively, the adult says, "You are a sensitive child." This is engraved in him. If tried to resolve it at the right time, he would have known how to divert his sensitivity and deal with the issue, but if care is provided all the time, not giving him a chance, he will remain a sensitive child, who is afraid of taking a chance. Over a period, these labels become internalized. The person does not see anxiety as an experience. They see it as themselves. The label becomes a lens through which they see themselves for the rest of their lives. "This is who I am." Period...

Reflection Exercise:

In your journal, list down all the labels or how I view myself:

- I am anxious
- I am a nervous cat.
- I am always stressed and nervous
- I am depressed all the time

Now read the statements and say them aloud to yourself, and note how you feel. Surely, not a good feeling.

Now, re-label yourself as:

- I feel anxious most of the time / sometimes
- I wish to do things perfectly, and I keep trying
- I feel low sometimes / I feel sad sometimes

"The aim is not to deny the struggle. Accept it, but do not make it an identity that we relate to or make it a personality. "

Living in suffering

Tell me one person who loves to live in suffering. I am sure none of us. But for someone who has identified themselves with pain or suffering, for them, suffering is a way of life. You may have heard a few people saying,

- "Suffering and I are sisters. We cannot live without each other. This is my life."
- Where there is pain, I am always there."
- Pain follows me everywhere"

It's not that pain has their address only. It's that these people have accepted suffering, pain, or anxiety as a part and parcel of their lives. They feel lost without it, as if their existence is at stake. They are born only to suffer. Anxiety becomes their second home, even if they are in a state of pain. Peace becomes suffocation for them.

Worry to prevent mishaps

Some people carry worry as if they are wearing jewellery. They believe that unless and until they worry, problems will occur and reoccur. The only way to prevent problems from happening is to worry. They associate worry as a lucky charm or an evil eye, swaying problems away. Tell them to stop worrying, and they will be buried under a mountain of problems. For them, worrying is caring and a responsibility that they proudly carry.

They believe:

- If I am worried, I am responsible
- If I worry, I am a caring person
- Most importantly, if I am worried, I am prepared....

The question here is whether worry really erases the problem? It is just a means of erasing peace. The peace required to challenge oneself to deal with the issue at hand.

Self-Protection

Humans are social animals, and the most important aspect for them is to be accepted in society. Fear or anxiety is a direct result of self-protection. Simply stated, one does not wish others to see their weakness, and hence they assume an identity. Fear is a means of protecting oneself from

- Fear of rejection
- Fear of loss
- Fear of failure

"What if due to my weakness, friends don't accept me?"

Honestly, at some point in time in life, this fear or self-acceptance has worked in the past. It has protected us from making mistakes. It helped avoid criticism or embarrassment. You may not have lost your temper easily, or you learned the art of gelling with all kinds of people. But is it a foolproof theory? It may have worked once. What is the guarantee that it will always work and in all situations? The brain learns, "This is the only way to keep me safe."

Fear generates another well-known issue, "Perfectionism. "One needs to be perfect to be accepted in the society. It is a well-known fact that no one can be perfect. Human nature is to flaw. So, perfectionism is nothing more than wearing a mask. But how long can you wear a mask? A mask composed of guilt and fear, keeping you on your toes, anxious that if anyone were to unleash the mask, the true self would be revealed. Perfectionism whispers, "Ifyou do everything perfectly, nobody can hurt you,and you will be accepted without fail."

Yet there is no guarantee. People will still blame or criticize, and you will be imperfect in someone's eyes. Being perfect is a game. It's like running on a treadmill, where there is no end. People assume perfectionism stems from ambition, but honestly, perfectionism stems from anxiety. The race to being perfect will never end, as anxiety runs behind you with a stick, saying, "There is scope for improvement. Go on."

A new Identity

When you begin healing, you create a new identity: "Who am I without anxiety"?

Many people feel lost without worry or fear, as it is their identity, and they avoid healing. As healing will destroy their identity. But anxiety is not your identity; it is an experience. Fear is an emotion and not your personality. First thing healing does is dissociate you from your identity. It's as simple as reframing the way you speak to yourself. Reframing your thoughts.

Instead of saying, "I am anxious," say, "I experience anxiety, but it is just an experience."

You are an observer of your thoughts and not the thoughts themselves. Your self-talk is what matters the most.

Healing means trusting yourself

It's not all about erasing fear. It's about dealing with it consciously and through proper channels. Fear does not define your moves. Confidence does not mean the absence of anxiety, but feeling the panic yet being able to move forward. Healing occurs when you associate with your values and not with your anxiety.

Simply say to yourself, "What matters to me, I will work on it" instead of saying, "What if I fail?"

Instead of "What people think of me." Say, "What kind of person do I wish to be?"

Reflection Exercise:

Journal the following:

Exercise 2: When did the story originate:

Sometimes, identity is something that we have inherited by being constantly labelled either with praise or criticism. Recall, who and when were you labelled or called:

- Perfectionist
- Shy
- Slow coach
- Sensitive / Shy

Situations and the reaction of others, especially an Adult / Parent towards you, labelling you, helped form your identity/personality.

This exercise should make you realize that, as a child, you were vulnerable and started relating to the labels.

Exercise 3: What am I afraid of:

Think of something that you are constantly struggling with.

Eg: "What if I fail?" is a constant worry.

Go deeper, till you find out the core fear.

It can be a failure associated with your past, where you

- Might have been called a failure
- Might have been rejected

Many of our fear/anxiety is associated with our self-worth and societal expectations.

Part 3

Part III:

THE POWER OF TODAY

VIII
The Power of Presence

"The Present is an antidote to depression and anxiety."

How... Read further to understand.

Life Missed / Abandoned

Imagine. You are living a fulfilled life. A beautiful house with all modern amenities. A loving and caring family, two-course meals, and everything that one could ask for to live happily. Yet, the mind keeps wandering over past issues that are not accomplished and the future uncertain events.

The mind keeps wandering between past failures or accomplishments and the future, "what if's, "not allowing you to experience the current moments. The mind constantly travels between yesterday and tomorrow. Meanwhile, the present moment is sitting quietly, awaiting its turn in the background. A moment that never arrives.

The Mind as a Time Machine

One of the most extraordinary talents we humans have is "mind travel," just like a time machine that helps people cross time, whether in the future or the past, but the mind has evolved so much that it does not require any machine to time-travel. It just needs to sit and wander.

At any moment:

- You can visit issues 10 years ago
- Replaying a conversation or a fight that happened years ago
- Imagining oneself 10 years from now
- Imagine what your retirement life will be.

It was this ability that helped our ancestors survive, and it is helping us now to deal with ourselves as well in uncertain situations by keeping us safe. It helps us learn from experience and plan for future challenges. But the ability that helps us survive also binds us into suffering. Simply because the mind does not understand the difference between visiting the past and living there, as well as planning for the future and living there, too.

The Past is pulling us backwards

Think what your mind replays:

- A relationship that has ended
- A conflict between family members
- A job lost/missed opportunity

The mind keeps returning to these memories. Memories that have happened way back in our past. Any idea why the mind keeps returning to these memories?

Eg, Imagine you have a project in hand. You research and get all your facts ready, yet you are uneasy. Thinking about what if somewhere you are lagging or missing something. You do this till you are certain that everything is to the point. You get closure as per your satisfaction. Unless and until you are satisfied, you do not leave it.

A similar analogy. Things have gone badly in your past. Something in it is left incomplete. You revisit them so that you get closure. A satisfactory answer or outcome. Yet, no matter how many times you revisit the past, the past won't change. The only thing that can be done is to gain experience and move on. Spending too much time in the past, we miss the present – Now.

Living in the past makes us emotional or sad. That is where depression steps in, pulling us backwards in a situation that cannot change. Depression or reliving the past is like stepping into a closed room where nothing can be changed.

The Future is pulling us forward

Future or Anxiety has a different language. Mainly, "What if?"

- What if I Fail?
- What if I lose everything
- What if things go wrong

Anxiety lives in the future, predicting what has never happened or predicting what will happen. Anxiety constantly aims to predict tomorrow or the future. The problem is that most of the time, what we worry about never happens. The idea is that the more you worry, the more you will create certainty or a solution to the issue, but certainty never arrives, and we keep dreaming and predicting.

Depression says, "Look behind."

Anxiety says: "Look ahead."

Presence says, "Look here."

The question here is, "Where are you looking"?

Define Presence?

Imagine driving on a busy road. You are driving while listening to the radio. Suddenly, a song takes you to the past or the future. What will happen to your driving? A sudden distraction from the present can cause an accident. Presence, in simple words, means paying attention to the now. It sounds simple, but one of the most difficult things to do. Being present does not mean ignoring the future or forgetting the past. It simply means not allowing either the past or the future to steal the present. In simple terms, Presence is simply not just doing extraordinary things, but doing ordinary things with awareness. Simply like:

- Watching our breath
- Noticing the taste of the food while eating

Presence seems difficult, and we resist it

One of the most difficult times to be in is in the present. Only because it contains facts and or reality. And nothing is more difficult than facing reality. Reality is where all the emotions are locked up in.

Eg, Someone lost a job due to the recession. Being in the present situation, what are his emotions? He is filled with grief, sadness, hopelessness, etc.

When people experience these emotions, they are heavy to deal with, and people search for means to escape. The only means to escape or move into a safer zone is by escaping into the past or the future. Anything feels easier than sitting in the present with those uncomfortable, piercing emotions. Yet avoiding these leads to unexpected issues. The problems exist; they are just postponed for the time being. Presence simply says face the issues without running or fighting them. We need to acknowledge it simply.

Presence simply means:

- Present and being sad
- Present and grieving
- Present and frustration

Presence says acknowledge your feelings. Instead of saying, "I shouldn't feel this way," say, "This is what I am feeling right now"

Psychological Timeline

Clocks, calendars, planners, etc., keep us updated about deadlines and time limits. But what is a psychological timeline? A psychological timeline is simply an emotional timeline. When someone is emotionally stuck in their past or their future and avoids the present. It creates a psychological or mental health issue, caging the person in their past or future timeline rather than the present.

Where does Healing happen?

Imagine being in a time machine. Imagine you have been given the magical wand to correct either your past or your future? Which one would you like to heal? Most people would heal the past so that the present and the future are taken care off. Wow... Life is beautiful, isn't it?

If only we had a time machine? Coming to the now. Being a human, given a magic wand, what would you like to heal? Past, present, or the future. Whatever you wish to heal, the answer is simple. You can heal only the present, the NOW.

Where does all the action happen? Where will healing work?

- Walking or having a conversation with a friend or loved one
- Score or marks
- Job promotion

It happens now, not in the past nor in the future. Even your memories were once present moments, and what you dream or aspire to will once be happening now, not in the future.

Past, as the word says, is past or over. How can we reach there physically to make changes? We can only reach the past in our imagination and imagine cleaning or healing, but is it practically possible?

Future, as the word says, means something that will occur or is yet to happen. So, something that has not happened, how can you change it or heal from it? So, it is obvious that life is happening now.

At this moment you are:

- Happy
- Working
- In a relationship

When all the actions are happening now, in the present, then healing can happen only in the present. It's like a wound or bleeding. Immediate action is needed. Immediate actions equals healing. You are bleeding now, so healing or bandage has to happen now, itself not later.

Conditional Happiness

One of the reasons people prefer being in the future is that it creates a comfortable picture. "Will be." This creates conditional happiness.

- I will be happy when my children grow up
- I will be happy when I own a house
- I will be happy when I get a promotion

This conditional happiness creates tension. This habit of postponing happiness is dangerous. It creates a void. It calls for a journey, whereby the destination is not important. The goal is important, and unless and until achieved, one is trapped in the future or past.

Returning to the Present

The mind is a wanderer. It will move freely from one timeline to the other. From the present to the past to the future. But one needs to hold on and bring back the mind to the present. The goal is to notice when it wanders and bring it back again and again without being judgmental. Every return strengthens the awareness, bringing you back to life.

Acceptance vs Retaliation

Thinking does not create or change reality. Accepting it and experiencing it creates reality.

Eg, You can think about the comfort from a warm cup of tea in a cold winter season. Whereas, holding and feeling the warmth from the cup leads to an experience that is a reality.

Resistance happens in the thought process, in which we do not accept reality. It may happen either in the past or in the future.

Acceptance says, "This is happening"

Whereas resistance says, "This should not have happened"

Note the minutest detail. After a situation happens, the guilt provokes a resistance, and one pushes themselves into a cocoon, whereas after the situation happens, if one accepts it, they get the zeal to find the solution and move ahead, gaining experience.

Acceptance is not a sign of weakness but a sign of wisdom. It is an understanding that reality does not change because we are fighting or we are guilty about it. The past will be intact whether we revisit it or not. The best is to accept it. Only then does learning happen, and based on the experience, our present follows. Acceptance allows us to accept life as it is and not waste our energy on lost battles, whereas resistance creates suffering and leads us to a never-ending battle.

A beautiful quote by Maxim Lagace, "Accept the chaos of life. Fools try to control it. The wise dance with it."

Reflection Exercise:

In your journal, make a note of:

Where does my mind spend most of its time?

- The past?
- The future?
- The present?

After a few minutes, notice:

- Five things you can see.
- Four things you can touch.
- Three things you can hear.
- Two things you can smell.
- One thing you are grateful for.

This simple exercise helps bring your attention back to the present moment.

A Letter from the Present Moment

If NOW could speak, it would say:

- I am where life is
- I am where your loved ones are
- I am where your joys are

Why do you keep searching for life in your past or future? When I am here with you all along....

IX

Small steps and your relationship with time.

A natural progression towards lasting change.

Change is an overwhelming process, and when changes happen all at once, it can be overwhelming. Change needs to happen one step at a time and over the course of time.

Struggling to Change

After reading about anxiety, depression, and acceptance, readers wish to change. But the question is, "How will I change?" Simply, it is not easy, yet steps need to be taken, but most importantly, by being in the present.

A person suffering from depression thinks, "I need to completely rebuild my life."

A person suffering from anxiety thinks, "I need to stop worrying forever."

When they see the distance between where they are and where they wish to be, they feel it is next to impossible to cover the distance and hence resist change.

Where is the future built?

Imagine someone who is obese and has enrolled in a weight loss program. The duration is 6 months long and may take longer as well. What will the person's reaction be? The person feels overwhelmed thinking about the end. What she sees is the journey instead of the next step.

Life works similarly. The future is not created tomorrow but by what we do today. Today's actions, habits, and choices define our tomorrow.

Our relationship with Time

Most of us are living either in the past or in the future. Dialogues like

- "When I start a business, I will be successful"
- I wish I had taken a different step
- When things get better
- One day....
- Someday...

Instead of today...

These dialogues are harmless, but the worst thing they do is postpone life and its happening. We treat life or the present moment as a waiting room. Waiting for something to happen. But real life never arrives in the future. It is happening now, at the moment itself. Coincidentally, when tomorrow comes, it happens in the present itself, making it life as happening now.

The overnight transformation

Successful stories are inspiring. The way the stories are portrayed shows as if success has happened overnight. No struggle or just a day's struggle and success touched them. No one knows or wishes to know the struggle behind their success. It's like a movie. The actor faces an issue, and just within 3 hours, a solution is found. Happy ending.

Big changes are small changes repeated consistently.

Imagine a toddler. A toddler before he starts to walk or stand upright. Do you remember the struggle? How many times have you fallen and cried for help? But did you give up? No. It was the continuous trying that helped you reach where you are at this moment. Standing upright and walking without a fall. Similarly, healing does not happen overnight. Growth is gradual. Small change, the first change is invisible, and hence people feel that despite the step taken, nothing has changed.

Baby Steps and healing

The mind underestimates gradual progress. We notice dramatic events and overlook the smaller ones. The anxious mind wants certainty, whereas the perfectionist self wants immediate results, and the depressed mind wants proof that things are working, but life does not certify any of these. Instead, it asks us to trust. Trust by taking small steps. One step at a time, holding on to the trust.

Eg. The person on a weight loss session. The person may have started dieting and exercising. Small steps taken, but initially, she may see no changes in her scale. Healing says, hold on to the process. Trust that change is happening and put in continuous efforts. Gradually, changes would be noticed. Give in time. Take the baby steps needed.

Similarly, healing happens gradually.

- One therapy session will not transform your life
- One mindful breath will not heal anxiety

But repeating it consistently will make profound changes.

The danger of waiting, but by being present

Presence is where healing happens. Many postpone healing because they are waiting. Waiting for that one motivation or one confidence to begin with. This would happen only when they are in the present situation. The perfect time rarely would arrive. One needs to strike for healing to happen. Don't wait for the right moment. Action taken is the right moment.

Healing and Questions to ask

Humans are impatient animals. They want quick results, and hence they ask their therapist:

- How long will it take to heal completely?

But for healing to happen, one needs to frame the question differently. "What should I do today for healing to happen?" Perhaps it is asking for patience, courage, honesty, or simply rest.

Whatever is the answer to healing? The answer will always be found in the present moment and not in the future that has not yet arrived. Hence, action happens in today's moment. Think of today for the futures' healing.

Reflection Exercise:

In your journal, write:

- What change am I hoping for?
- What future outcome am I looking for?
- What is one small step I can take today?

Now complete the statement and repeat it to yourself:
"Today, the next right step for me is ___."

X

Build a Life in the Present

The goal is neither to eliminate the past nor erase the future, but to build a life in the present. The NOW moment. Easier said than done.

A simple analogy explaining that life is happening at the moment itself.

We all have heard of death on the spot, accidental death, or suicide. Where is life? It is gone forever. Now, think whether the person who passed away, where was the person in – The past or the future? Nowhere. Life was happening and ended abruptly. Now, think if the person who passed away was only thinking of his past or his future? Was he or she living? Was life having any meaning for him? Death teaches us the value of life. A life that happens only now. Death chases and stops everything immediately.

Existing vs Living:

Let's start with an easy question. Are we existing or living?

The day-to-day chores we do, job, children, opportunities, vacation, functions, relationship, retirement, and old age, ending with death. It's a life cycle each one of us goes through. Is this living or existing? Now, in every phase of life, add experience, pay attention, and live every moment. Notice the difference. This is the difference between living and existing. Existing means attendance in a class or office, whereas living means simply adding meaning to every moment.

What are you doing? Existing or living?

Circle of Life to be in the Present

As said, life is a circle. Where you start, you end up at the same point. As said, life cannot happen in the future nor the past, a waiting room syndrome. If you wait for something good to happen to enjoy life, you will just keep waiting or simply keep hoping. Because when that happens, the future becomes the present, and then you keep waiting for the next one to happen. Unable to enjoy the moment.

Think, what does a child want from you? Or as a child, what did you demand from your parents? We all have heard statements from a child saying, "My parents have no time for me." What do they mean here?

Simply: Attention

Imagine you are giving a presentation in an auditorium, and the audience is busy speaking or talking amongst themselves. How would you feel? Would the presentation have any value? This is life.

Life is a reel, continuously playing. Yet, you don't pay attention, and the focus is shifted. So instead of reliving the moment, we are focused somewhere in the past or the future. Are we enjoying life, the moment, or are we cribbing about correcting the past or something not achieved? Pay attention and see the difference.

Friendship with Self

Imagine someone who stops you from wandering here and there. Stopping you from focusing too much on past issues or future events? Would that be helpful? Indeed. At least you would focus on the NOW. That someone is none other than your inner voice. A friend who will think only of your good. The friend is aware of your movements and can stop you immediately, bringing you back into the present. The voice is like a teacher who stops you immediately from wandering about, bringing you back to life and enjoying it.

"The goal is not to visit the present occasionally but to build a memorable life there itself."

Part 4

Part IV:

SENSE AND SENSIBILITY

XI

Senses - A Bridge between You and the World

Have you ever wondered how we connect with the world? How are experiences formed? How do we get or how are we a storehouse of information?

From the time the child is born, the child is making or forming connections.

- Why does the child cry initially after birth?
- How does it know who their parents are / sibling?

The answer is simple. The Senses.

Our 5 senses – Eyes, Ears, Nose, Smell, and Touch help us gather information that helps connect easily with the world around us. In a newborn child, the sense of touch is primary. When they are left alone, they are insecure, and they cry. When the mother holds the child, they feel safe and connected. With the help of other senses, they connect deeper. With the help of sight, they know the features of the mother, followed by the other means of association.

The senses act as a bridge between the vast information and experiences connected with it.

- How do you know whether the tone of the person is rude or pleasant?
- How do you know the cup is hot or cold?
- How do you differentiate between danger and being safe?

Few instances. While crossing the road, it was the sense of sight that taught you how to cross the road safely. That is how it has been registered in your memory. It need not be taught to you again and again. It has become a habit. A naturally occurring habit.

Learning happens through the senses:

- Visual Learning – Learning by Sight -Eyes
- Auditory Learning. – Learning by listening – Ears
- Tactile learning – Learning by touching – Touch / Feeling
- Olfactory learning – Learning by smelling – Nose
- Learning through taste – Tongue

Learning can be through any one of the senses or through a combination of the senses. Mostly, we learn through a combination of the senses, but one of them is a primary mode of learning.

Not going deeper into the senses. Let's come to the crucial point.

Why from the past, present, and future, have I jumped to the senses?

As a layman, we believe that senses work in the presence. True. Yet from a psychological perspective, the senses connect our learning to our past learning and experiences.

Eg, We do not learn a language every day. Or we do not learn about danger or crossing the road safely every day. One time we learned it, and it has been registered, and based on the current scenario, we take the necessary steps.

As psychologists say, "Senses are not neutral. They keep pulling us from the past to the present to the future. They are constantly feeding information to the brain. The brain then attaches meaning to the said information through what experiences are stored from the past." This is the basic part of it, which helps in survival, but the issue is the stage of stagnation. A stage where one is stuck, whether in the past or the future. This is where the living stops, and the person either enters the depression or anxiety phase, which, if it exists for a shorter period of time, is fine, but if it is a daily affair, it can be harmful.

As said, "The past is a memory, so the past lives in the sensory memory. Future is based on imagination, and hence the future is based on sensory imagination, while the present is based on experience, and hence the present is based on sensory experience."

Retreating to the Past – Senses leading to depression

- A smell or a perfume reminds you of the lost person
- A song reminds you of someone
- The smell or taste of a delicacy reminds you of your mother or grandmother
- A place or a ride reminds you of the happy moments spent together with a loved one

All these are common occurrences. I am sure that each one of us has dropped a tear experiencing one or many of these or other situations. Dropping a tear or experiencing tear-jerking moments leads to an emotional moment or sadness. When sadness stays for a longer period, it may turn into depression. But the question is, are these memories or the past causing emotional distress? Observe the moment. It is the experience or the meaning associated with the memory that creates a vacuum when someone revisits the past, which leads to depression or moments of sadness. Memories are like a picture. It is the experience associated with it through our senses that causes distress.

Why do memories lead to depression?

As said before, it is not the memory, but the experience associated with it that creates the emotional turmoil. But think about why it leads to depression? Or why does a person get stuck at a time, not wishing to move ahead or come back to the moment? Experience associated with the memory can be both good and bad. We relive both depending on the current situation. When the current situation is disturbing, we tend to retreat to the good old experiences.

Someone who is experiencing high-level stress in their job and feels broken. He then tries to calm himself and retreats to the happy-go-carefree days. Being there relieved he comes back with a zeal to fight the workload stress, but someone who retreats to the comfort zone of the past as an escape mechanism from the current stressful situation is at psychological risk.

Another reason why someone retreats to their comfort zone in the past is when they seek closure. Something has happened in the past. We have moved ahead, but the present situation demands closure. Again, the mind wanders, pricking the senses for the experience demanding an answer, but is the answer found?

Eg, When a close one dies. You have not been speaking to them for ages. Now, after the death of that person, memories come back haunting you. Now the question is not who committed the mistake, but guilt. You want one last word with that person, but alas, the person is no more. At this junction, the mind pricks the senses for happy moments spent with that person. The happier days. Most common during the mourning phases.

The person is no longer experiencing the present. They are emotionally reliving the past. The issue here is coming back to life at the present, which sometimes some people don't, as being in a comfort zone is pleasant than uncertainty or a stressful life. Hence, memory or living in the past is associated with sensory experience, creating an illusion enveloping the person into depression. Action needs to be taken immediately by asking your senses to come back to the present. Seeking medical help is advisable when the situation is out of hand.

Fear of the unknown future – Senses leading to anxiety

Anxiety works differently. Instead of activating experiences, it starts predicting outcomes. A general or common statement by someone anxious is:

- "What will happen"
- What if"
- I don't know what to do"

It is uncertainty. A prediction misguides a person into the clutches of fear and panic. It's like a movie but playing in fast-forward motion.

Eg, A real-life scenario that happened or is happening with a dear friend of mine. Her son is in Grade 8th. Maharashtra state came up with the compulsory 3rd language for the boards. Whether the rule has been implemented by the school or not, or changes have been made by the board, she panicked about her son's future. The fear went to an extent that she started feeling pain sensations all over her body, and in fear, would wake up in the middle of the night, sweating. The boy had 3 years to go, and lots of things can change by that time. Or if the rule had been implemented, she could have managed for tuition, but before any closure, she panicked, and fear made her anxious.

What happens here is that the situation has been imagined. The danger is yet to come, but the mind, through the help of senses, connects it with a similar situation, and the body reacts.

In the above example. The friend of mine recalled a situation in which she was in a similar situation. She was in 10th, and the syllabus changed. Also, reading about the experiences of other students in newspapers, she related the incidents to her son's future and started fearing and panicking.

The Brain and Association

Whether the past experience or future fear, the brain learns through association. The main work of the senses is to associate with a person or an event, and that's how we remember.

Song + heartbreak or Loss

Think of a time when you sang a duet with your loved one. Today, the song may remind you of that moment, and you miss your partner. You have associated the song with your loved one. Either a heartbreak situation or the loss of a person due to death.

Hospital + Fear

Hospitals are generally associated with loss. Generally, you visit a hospital or take your loved ones to the hospital when there is a health issue. Running behind tests and treatments instils fear of the unknown. You don't know the outcome and associate the hospital with fear. It can be due to the painful treatment process you had to go through or the loss of a loved one.

Senses – The Culprit

The question here is, "Is sense the culprit?" Senses are not an issue, but the association created with the senses. The smell, taste, or sight is not the culprit. They are the ones absorbing the issue, and through associations, they get stored in the form of experiences that ignite when a situation occurs that needs closure or an answer. The senses collect information and starts forming an association. Memory turns the information into the past, while imagination turns the information into the future.

Lines to ponder on:

- A smell is just a smell until memory makes it yesterday.
- A sound is just a sound until fear makes it tomorrow.

The senses are often the doorway guiding the mind to enter the three worlds.

Part 5

Part V:

Healing through our Senses

XII

Returning home through the 5 senses

Depression pulls us into the past, while Anxiety often pulls us into the future. The mind wanders from the past to the future. While we are aware that healing happens in the present. The question is, how do we stop the mind from wandering back and forth?

Since senses are responsible for the mind to wander, it is the senses that can help heal, too.

The mind can time-travel. It can wander 10 years into the past, reliving a past, and at the same time wander 10 years into the future. It can predict the worst situation, creating panic. From the above, what do we conclude? Simple. Is it the mind or the senses? The answer is simple.

The mind. It is the mind that wanders from one place to another. Senses are intact and not moving.

Imagine yourself in a place that you visited a few years ago with a loved one. The mind wanders back to that place, but where are your senses? Your eyes can see the wall where there is a photo frame, or your ears can hear the birds chirping at your window. Notice, sense whether eyes, ears, or touch is the fastest way to connect to the present, not the mind.

The mind wanders, whereas your body is living in the present or in the moment. The mind travels. Every physical sensation is an invitation to return to the present.

Whenever you feel your mind wanders, try the 5 to 1 exercise

- 5 things I can see?
- 4 things I can hear?
- 3 things I can feel?
- 2 things I can taste?
- 1 thing I can smell?

This simple exercise will help bring the mind back into reality.

Finally.

The past is a memory, whereas the future is filled with possibilities. The present is a gift. Keep unwrapping the gifts called life by being in the present.

"Welcome Home" simply by using the train metaphor

- Yesterday's train still arrives.
- Tomorrow's train still arrives.

But you don't need to board the train. You can wait at the platform itself, simply observing your thoughts. Observe the thoughts without becoming the thought. Remember the past as a moving memory without living there. Prepare for the future without fearing it. Keep your senses on high alert like a friend who holds you before you stumble and fall.

"Happy Living with all your senses in action."

THE WORDS OF WISDOM

Before I end the book, though there is a lot to be said, but one word of wisdom I would leave with my readers is that, "This is a Self-help book," not therapy or counseling itself.

The difference is as simple as self-medication vs visiting a GP or a speialist r simply a doctor. I do agree that no one other than yo yourself know theyself the best, yet there are times when approaching others, especially a specialised person, for help is not a sign of weakness but a sign of loving oneself. Self-help works beautifully unless and until one gets into its chronic form, mainly identifying with it or it affects daily chores.

The book has simple, daily, well-known steps that each one of us should follow, whether we are suffering or not. There is no harm in journaling about ourselves. It's like meditation, whereby instead of just focusing on your breathing, you focus on the thoughts that guide you completely.

Another and most important word of wisdom is don't ignore the book, thinking that none of this relates to me. Yes, I agree and pray that no one ever suffers from chronic depression or anxiety, but agree or not each one of us has mood changes and symptoms like sadness and restlessness or panic that we can control and get back to normal living. Yet, there is no harm in knowing situations that can cause depression or anxiety symptoms in the future. It's like being cautious well in advance.

Just like health, make mental health a priority as well.

Hope you are journaling every day....

www.ingramcontent.com/pod-product-compliance
Lightning Source LLC
LaVergne TN
LVHW022021200926
848481LV00007B/2464
* 9 7 9 8 9 0 5 6 0 2 9 9 3 *